PIANO SOLO

Disney
DUMBO

Music from the Motion Picture Soundtrack
Music by Danny Elfman

The following song is the property of:

Bourne Co. Music Publishers
www.bournemusic.com

BABY MINE

The following song in this publication is co-published by Bourne Co.:

TRAIN'S A COMIN'
(contains a portion of "CASEY JUNIOR")

ISBN 978-1-5400-5455-5

HAL•LEONARD®

Visit Hal Leonard Online at
www.halleonard.com

Contact us:
Hal Leonard
7777 West Bluemound Road
Milwaukee, WI 53213
Email: info@halleonard.com

In Europe, contact:
Hal Leonard Europe Limited
42 Wigmore Street
Marylebone, London, W1U 2RN
Email: info@halleonardeurope.com

In Australia, contact:
Hal Leonard Australia Pty. Ltd.
4 Lentara Court
Cheltenham, Victoria, 3192 Australia
Email: info@halleonard.com.au

TRAIN'S A COMIN'
Contains a portion of "Casey Junior"

Written by DANNY ELFMAN,
NED WASHINGTON and FRANK CHURCHILL

COLOSSEUM

Music by DANNY ELFMAN

MEET THE FAMILY

Music by DANNY ELFMAN

STAMPEDE!

Music by DANNY ELFMAN

BABY MINE

(As performed by Sharon Rooney)

Words by NED WASHINGTON
Music by FRANK CHURCHILL

DUMBO'S THEME

Music by DANNY ELFMAN

CLOWNS 1

Music by DANNY ELFMAN

DUMBO SOARS

Music by DANNY ELFMAN

HAPPY DAYS

Music by DANNY ELFMAN

COLETTE'S THEME

Music by DANNY ELFMAN

Moderately, expressively

mp

Pedal ad lib. throughout

CLOWNS 2

Music by DANNY ELFMAN

Moderate March

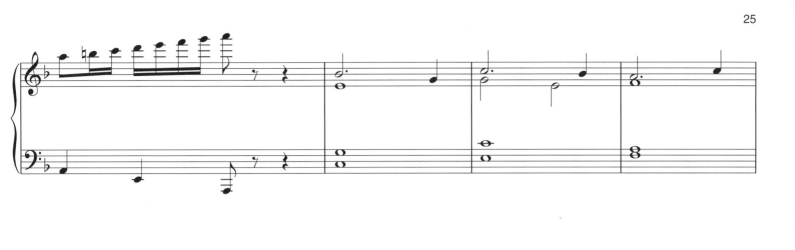

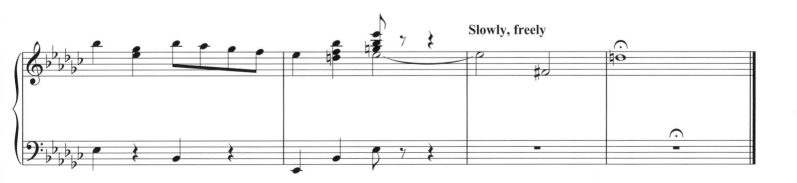

MEDICI CIRCUS – MIRACLES CAN HAPPEN

Music by DANNY ELFMAN

Moderately, in 1

Pedal ad lib. to end

BABY MINE
(As performed by Arcade Fire)

Words by NED WASHINGTON
Music by FRANK CHURCHILL

Waltz Ballad

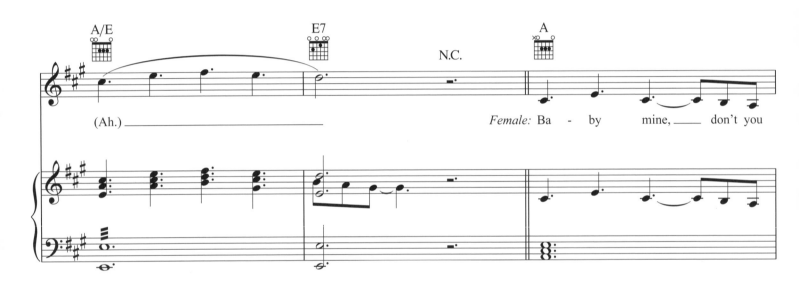

(Ah.) _____ *Female:* Ba - by mine, _____ don't you

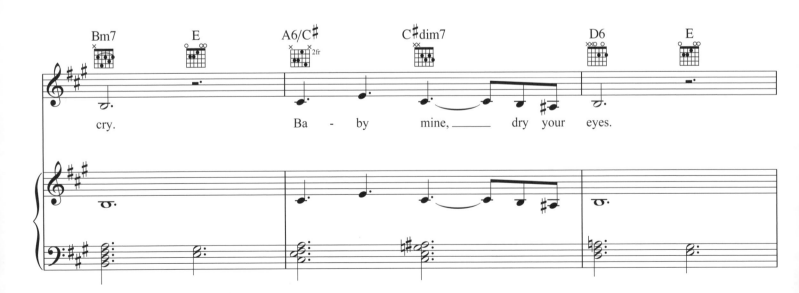

cry. Ba - by mine, _____ dry your eyes.

THE FINAL CONFRONTATION

Music by DANNY ELFMAN